POP HITS FOR THE TEEN PLAYER

EASY PIANO ARRANGEMENTS BY DAN COATES

W9-COV-205

Project Manager: Carol Cuellar
Art Layout: Joe Klucar

ALL I HAVE TO GIVE

Words and Music by
FULL FORCE
Arranged by DAN COATES

Moderately slow, with a steady beat

Verse 2:
When you talk, does it seem like he's not
Even listening to a word you say?
That's okay, baby, just tell me your problems.
I'll try my best to kiss them all away.
Does he leave when you need him the most
'Cause his friends get all your time?
Baby, please, I'm on my knees
Praying for the day that you'll be mine.
(To Chorus:)

AS LONG AS YOU LOVE ME

Words and Music by
MAX MARTIN
Arranged by DAN COATES

Moderately slow, with a steady beat

...BABY ONE MORE TIME

Words and Music by
MAX MARTIN
Arranged by DAN COATES

BACK AT ONE

Words and Music by
BRIAN McKNIGHT
Arranged by DAN COATES

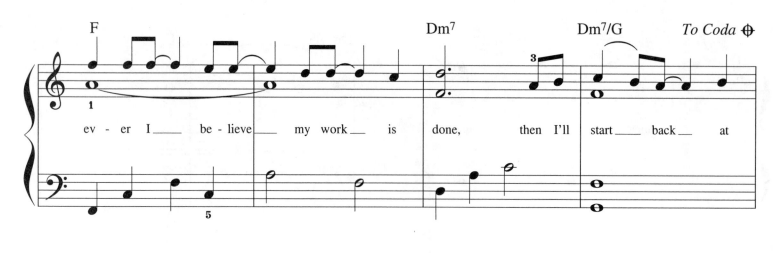

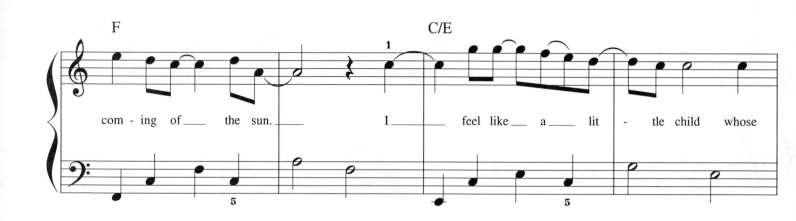

Em · Am · Dm⁷

lone - ly heart ___ of mine. _____ You threw out ___ the life - line, just
cresc.

G⁷sus⁴ · G⁷ · D.S. 𝄋 al Coda · Coda

in the nick ___ of time. _____ one. _____
dim.

mp · rit. · p

Verse 2:
It's so incredible,
The way things work themselves out.
And all emotional
Once you know what it's all about.
And undesirable
For us to be apart.
I never would have made it very far,
'Cause you know you've got the keys to my heart.
(To Chorus:)

BECAUSE OF YOU

Words and Music by
ANDERS BAGGE, ARNTHOR BIRGISSON,
CHRISTIAN KARLSSON and PATRICK TUCKER
Arranged by DAN COATES

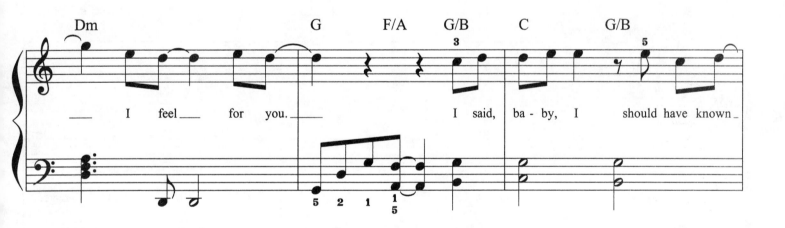

Verse 2:
Honestly, could it be you and me
Like it was before, need less or more?
'Cause when I close my eyes at night,
I realize that no one else
Could ever take your place.
I still can feel, and it's so real,
When you're touching me,
Kisses endlessly.
It's just a place in the sun
Where our love's begun.
I miss you,
Yes, I miss you.
(To Chorus:)

(YOU DRIVE ME) CRAZY

Words and Music by JORGEN ELOFSSON,
DAVID KREUGER, PER MAGNUSSON and
MAX MARTIN
Arranged by DAN COATES

(You Drive Me) Crazy - 4 - 1

To Coda ⊕

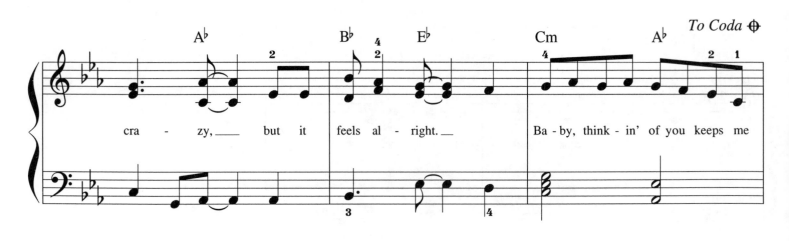

cra - zy, ___ but it feels al - right. ___ Ba - by, think - in' of you keeps me

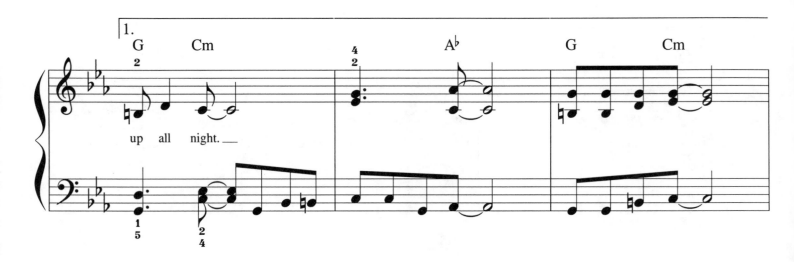

up all night. ___

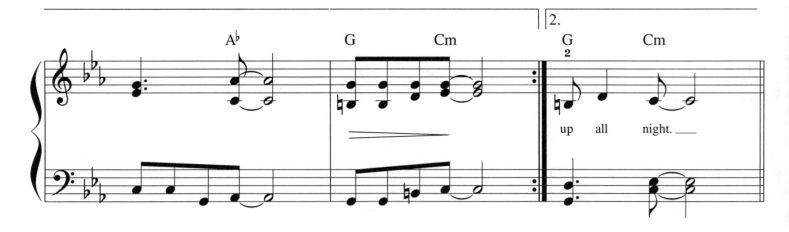

up all night. ___

Cra - zy, ___ I just can't sleep. ___ I'm so ex - cit - ed, I'm

GENIE IN A BOTTLE

Words and Music by
PAMELA SHEYNE, DAVID FRANK
and STEVE KIPNER
Arranged by DAN COATES

I DO (CHERISH YOU)

Words and Music by
KEITH STEGALL and **DAN HILL**
Arranged by DAN COATES

Moderately slow

(with pedal)

(L.H. simile)

1. All I am, all I'll be, ev-'ry-thing in this world, all that I'll ev-er need is in your eyes, shin-ing at me. When you smile

I Do (Cherish You) - 4 - 1

Verse 2:
In my world before you,
I lived outside my emotions.
Didn't know where I was going
Till that day I found you.
How you opened my life
To a new paradise.

In a world torn by change,
Still, with all of my heart
Till my dying day,
I do cherish you.   *(To Chorus:)*

I KNEW I LOVED YOU

Words and Music by
DARREN HAYES and
DANIEL JONES
Arranged by DAN COATES

36

I Knew I Loved You - 4 - 3

I WANT IT THAT WAY

Words and Music by
MAX MARTIN and ANDREAS CARLSSON
Arranged by DAN COATES

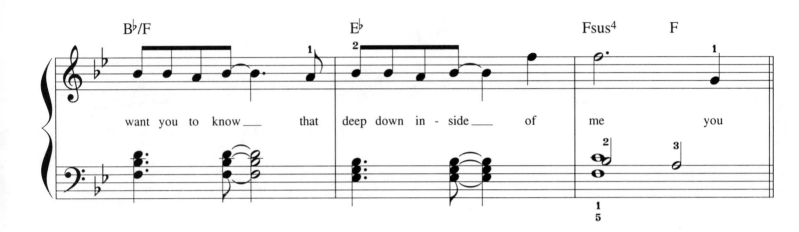

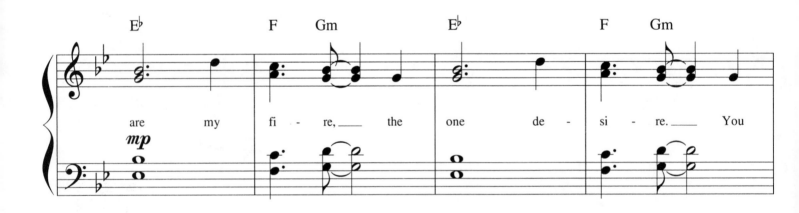

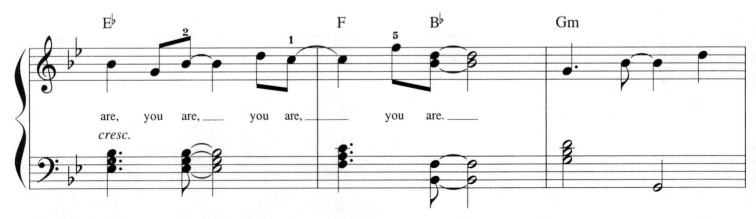

Verse 3:
Am I your fire,
Your one desire?
I know it's too late,
But I want it that way.
(To Chorus:)

I'LL NEVER BREAK YOUR HEART

By
ALBERT MANNO and
EUGENE WILDE
Arranged by DAN COATES

Verse 2:
As I walked by you,
Will you get to know me
A little more better?
Girl, that's the way love goes.
And I know you're afraid
To let your feelings show,
And I understand.
But girl, it's time to let go.
I deserve a try, honey,
Just once,
Give me a chance
And I'll prove this all wrong.
You walked in,
You were so quick to judge.
But, honey, he's nothing like me.
(To Chorus:)

LARGER THAN LIFE

Words and Music by
MAX MARTIN, KRISTIAN LUNDIN
and BRIAN T. LITTRELL
Arranged by DAN COATES

Steady rock beat ♩ = 120

Verse:

1. I may run and hide when you're scream-in' my name,___ al - right.
2. Look - in' at the crowd and I see your bod - y sway, come on.

But let me tell you now there are pric - es to fame,___ al -
Wish - in' I could thank you in a dif - fer - ent way,___ come

Larger Than Life - 4 - 1

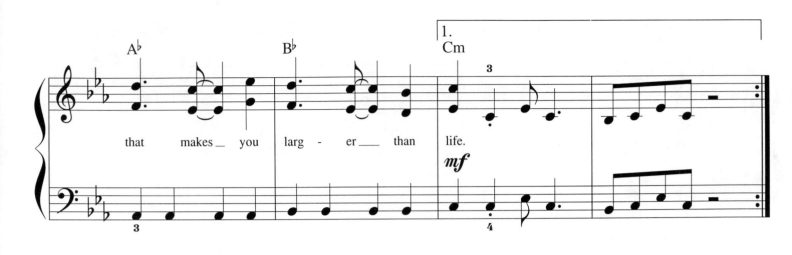

that makes____ you larg - er____ than life.

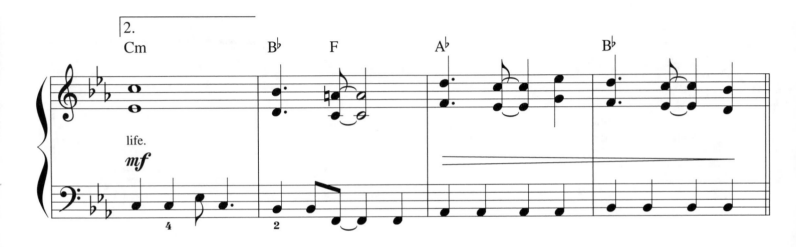

life.

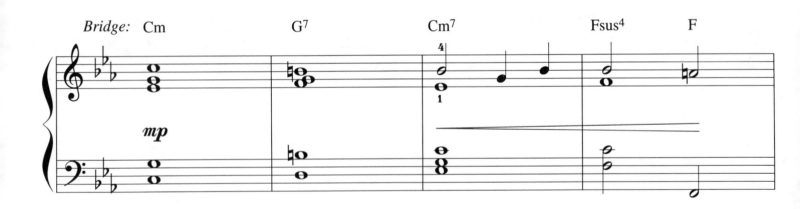

Bridge:

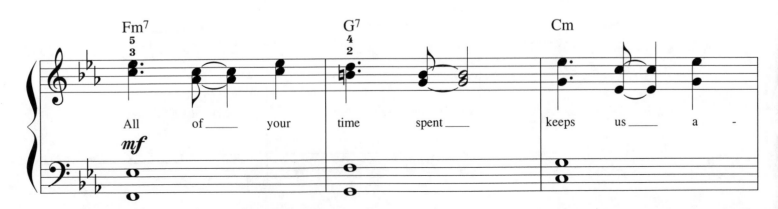

All of ____ your time spent____ keeps us ____ a -

(GOD MUST HAVE SPENT)
A LITTLE MORE TIME ON YOU

Words and Music by
CARL STURKEN and EVAN ROGERS
Arranged by DAN COATES

Gently, with expression

(God Must Have Spent) a Little More Time on You - 4 - 1

(God Must Have Spent) a Little More Time on You - 4 - 2

(God Must Have Spent) a Little More Time on You - 4 - 4

LIVIN' LA VIDA LOCA

Words and Music by
ROBI ROSA and DESMOND CHILD
Arranged by DAN COATES

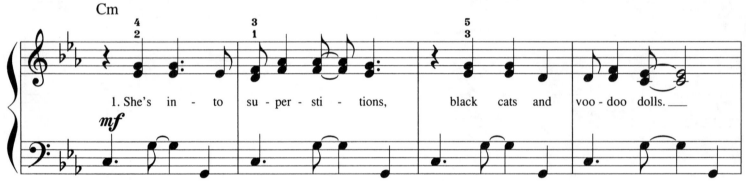

1. She's in-to su-per-sti-tions, black cats and voo-doo dolls.__

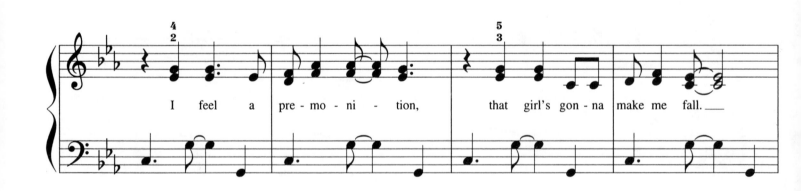

I feel a pre-mo-ni-tion, that girl's gon-na make me fall.__

Livin' La Vida Loca - 6 - 1

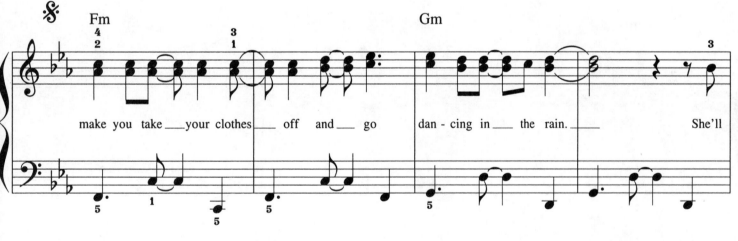

il red and her skin's the col - or of mo - cha._____

She will ____ wear ____ you out, liv - in' la vi - da lo -

ca, liv - in' la vi - da lo - ca. She's

liv - in' la vi - da lo - ca._____

Verse 3:
Woke up in New York City
In a funky, cheap hotel.
She took my heart and she took my money.
She must have slipped me a sleeping pill.

She never drinks the water
And makes you order French champagne.
Once you've had a taste of her
You'll never be the same.
Yeah, she'll make you go insane.
(To Chorus:)

From the Miramax Motion Picture "Music Of The Heart"
MUSIC OF MY HEART

Words and Music by
DIANE WARREN
Arranged by DAN COATES

Slowly, with feeling

(with pedal)

1. You'll nev - er know _____ what you've
2. You were the one _____ al - ways

done for me, _____ what your faith in me has
on my side, _____ al - ways stand - ing by,

done for my soul. _____ You'll nev - er know ___ the gift you've
see - ing me through. _____ You were the song ___ that al - ways

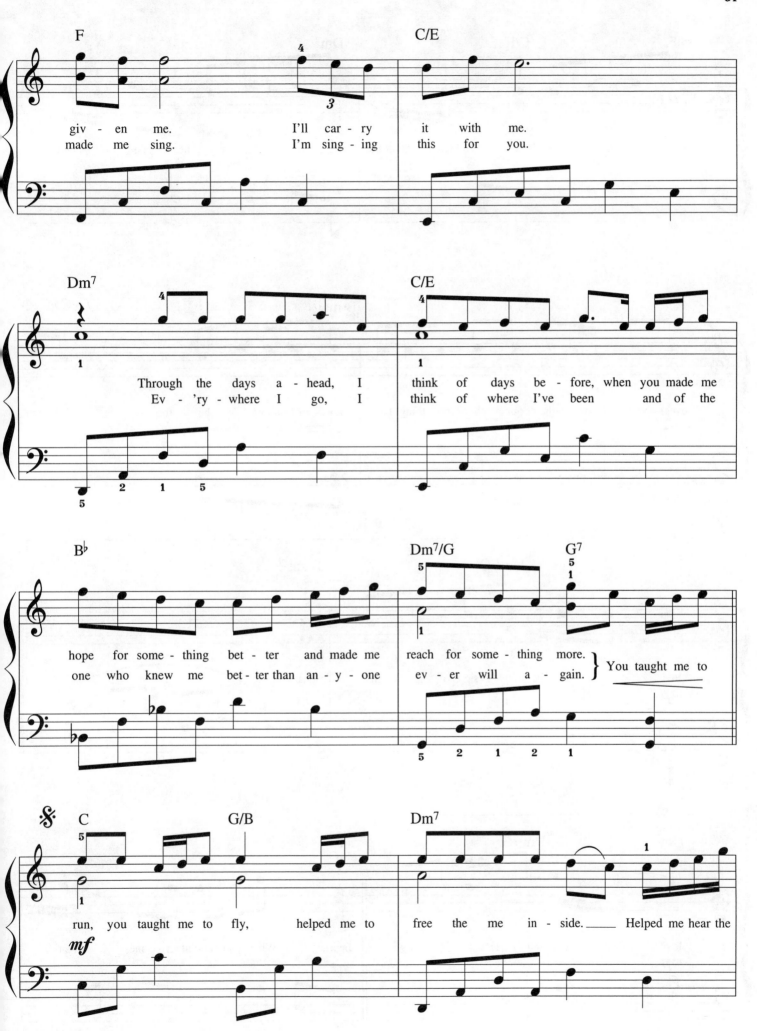

QUIT PLAYING GAMES
(With My Heart)

Words and Music by
MAX MARTIN and **HERBERT CRICHLOW**
Arranged by DAN COATES

Bright rock tempo

66

SHE'S ALL I EVER HAD

Words and Music by
ROBI ROSA, GEORGE NORIEGA
and JON SECADA
Arranged by DAN COATES

She's All I Ever Had - 4 - 1

SOMETIMES

Words and Music by
JORGEN ELOFSSON
Arranged by DAN COATES

Sometimes - 4 - 1

From the Twentieth Century-Fox Motion Picture "STAR WARS"

STAR WARS
(Main Title)

Music by
JOHN WILLIAMS
Arranged by DAN COATES

THAT'S THE WAY IT IS

Words and Music by
MAX MARTIN, KRISTIAN LUNDIN
and ANDREAS CARLSSON
Arranged by DAN COATES

WHEREVER YOU GO

Words and Music by
DURELL BOTTOMS, NICOLE RENEE
and MICHAEL McCRARY
Arranged by DAN COATES

Since you left___ me, my life

Wherever You Go - 6 - 1

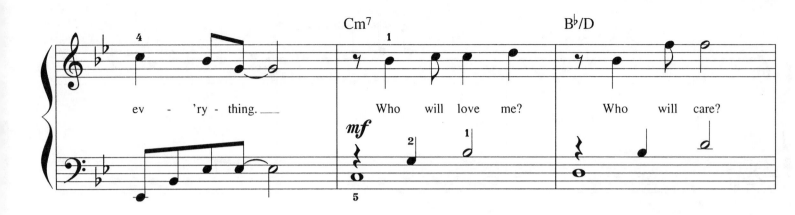

ev - 'ry - thing.____ Who will love me? Who will care?

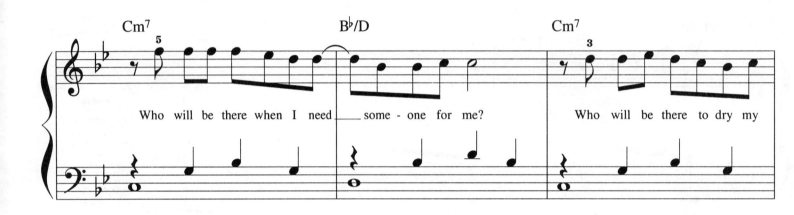

Who will be there when I need____ some - one for me? Who will be there to dry my

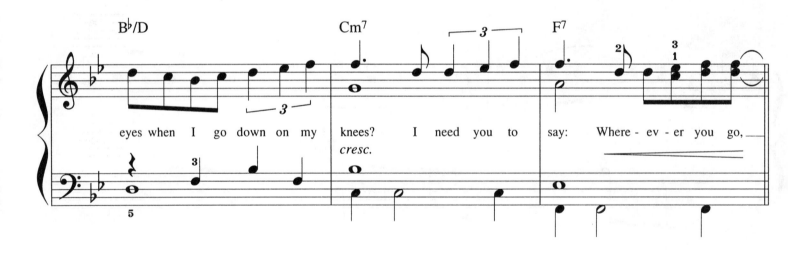

eyes when I go down on my knees? I need you to say: Where - ev - er you go,____

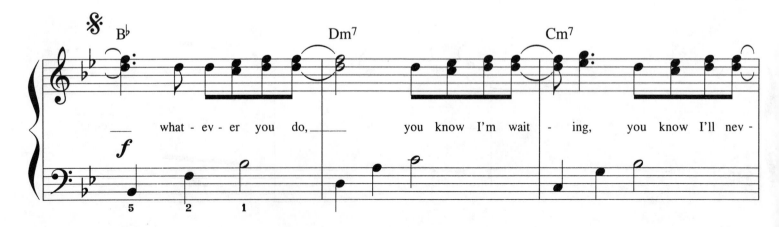

what - ev - er you do,____ you know I'm wait - ing, you know I'll nev -

Verse 2:
Goodbye is such a hard thing to say
When you're all I know,
When you're my everything.
And who will stay and care for me?
When you're gone, I'll be all alone.
Who will come and comfort me
And fulfill my needs?
Who will love me?
Who will care?
Who will be there
When I need someone for me?
Who will be there to dry my eyes
When I go down on my knees?
I need you to say:
(To Chorus:)

BAILAMOS

Words and Music by
PAUL BARRY and MARK TAYLOR
Arranged by DAN COATES

world in ___ out - side; don't let a mo - ment ___ go by. ___
leav - ing ___ your side; we're gon - na dance through __ the night. ___

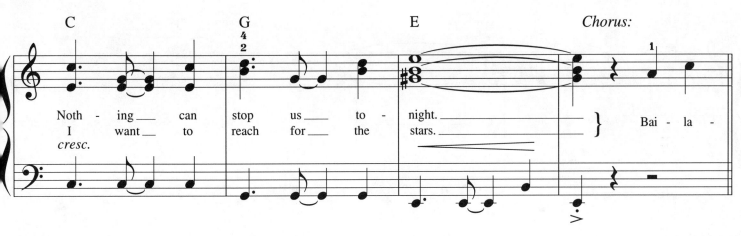

Chorus:

Noth - ing ___ can stop us ___ to - night. ___ Bai - la -
I want ___ to reach for ___ the stars. ___
cresc.

mos, ___ let the rhy - thm take __ you o - ver, bai - la -

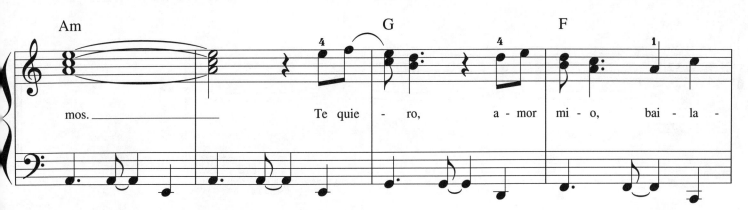

mos. ___ Te quie - ro, a - mor mi - o, bai - la -

mos. _____ Wan - na live this night ___ for - ev -

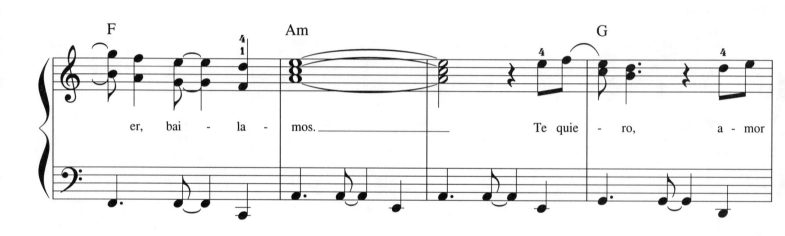

er, bai - la - mos. _____ Te quie - ro, a - mor

mi - o, te quie - ro. _____